W9-BNT-832

NEW YORK'S

5O BEST

NEW YORK'S
50 BEST

PLACES
TO
HAVE
BRUNCH

Ann Volkwein
& Jason Oliver Nixon

Illustrations by
Madeline Sorel

A CITY & COMPANY GUIDE
NEW YORK

Copyright © 1999 by Ann Volkwein and Jason Oliver Nixon
All rights reserved. No portion of this book may be reproduced
without written permission from the publisher.

Cover and text of Places to Have Brunch
Copyright © 1999 by Don Wise & Co.
Illustrations copyright © 1999 by Madeline Sorel

Library of Congress Cataloging-in-Publication Data
Volkwein, Ann.
New York's 50 best places to have brunch / Ann Volkwein
& Jason Oliver Nixon.
p.cm.
Includes index.
ISBN 1-885492-69-3

1.   Restaurants—New York (State)—New York Guidebooks.   2. New York (N.Y.)
Guidebooks.   I. Nixon, Jason Oliver.   II. Title.
TX907.3.N72N4862 1999
647.95747' 1—dc21   99-35442
                                                     CIP

PUBLISHER'S NOTE:
Neither City & Company nor the authors have any interest, financial or personal, in the
locations listed in this book. No fees were paid or services rendered in exchange for inclu-
sion in these pages. While every effort was made to ensure that information was accurate
at the time of publication, we recommend calling ahead to verify locations, prices, and
hours of operation. All area codes are 212 unless otherwise noted. Recipes were provid-
ed by the restaurants indicated.

10 9 8 7 6 5 4 3 2 1

Contents

Introduction

*B*runch is a meal that can be hard to describe. A character on *The Simpsons* summed it up this way: "It's not quite breakfast and it's not quite lunch, but it's filling, and it comes with a slice of cantaloupe on the side." Yes, but. Brunch encompasses much more than food. It's a loose-fitting term for any meal that occurs predinnertime, usually on the weekend, yet one that somehow transcends the feeling of "lunch." It might be omelets and hash browns at a diner at 11 A.M. on a Saturday morning with a friend. Or it could be a suit-and-tie affair with relatives at a posh hotel dining room at 1 P.M. Or it might be a midafternoon egg-filled popover in a delightful garden with a date. The venues, cuisines, and degrees of formality are infinite.

*N*ew York is a city with enviable and endless variations on the brunch theme. It may well be the most fertile ground for brunch in the world. Maybe it's the frenetic pace of life in this town that requires at least one meal a week with flexible hours and plenty of time to linger over coffee and chat with friends. Brunch persuades even the most hard-core New Yorkers to take a stress break in the softer atmosphere of a cafe or restaurant, every weekend.

*B*etween us, we have lived in nearly every neighborhood in Manhattan and eaten brunch in all of them, so when we started this book we had already visited many of the city's finest weekend eateries. Still, there were plenty of restaurants that we had heard were good but had never tried. Others that we knew to be exceptionally popular did not live up to our expectations. Over the course of a year we ate our way around the city, gained a few pounds, and eventually whittled our working list down to "50 best." Believe us, the whittling was the toughest part of the job.

*W*ithin this book, you'll find a wide range of cuisines—from French bistro fare to Korean barbecue, from Midwestern comfort food to Chinese dumplings. You will also find a price range for every budget, and ambiences to suit everyone's taste— from an Alphabet City hipster to an Upper East Side family and everything in between.

$	Under $12
$$	$12 to $18
$$$	$19 to $25
$$$$	Over $25

Balthazar

80 SPRING STREET AT CROSBY STREET
965-1414
SATURDAYS AND SUNDAYS, 11:30 A.M.—4 P.M.
RESERVATIONS ACCEPTED.
$$
AMEX, V, MC

With its pewter bar, vintage silver mirrors, and lush red leather banquettes, Balthazar is a masterful recreation of a Parisian brasserie. Dinner reservations are a near impossibility, so trendy is this venue, but brunch is another matter entirely.

While perusing the menu, enjoy peasant bread slathered with farm-fresh sweet butter. Consider one of Balthazar's several "hangover drinks," like Oyster Mary, a very spicy Bloody Mary served with a toothpick-skewered tender oyster resting on the rim of the glass. Order a plateau de fruits de mer, an artfully arranged assortment of bluepoint and West Coast oysters, littleneck clams on the half shell, and crab and lobster. Unusual egg

In the Neighborhood

Balthazar Bakery for take-out pastry and some confiture; west on Spring Street to the heart of SoHo with its shops and art galleries; the **Guggenheim Museum SoHo**, the **New Museum of Contemporary Art**, and the **Museum for African Art**, all on Broadway bet. Prince ➤

concoctions include eggs Meurette (poached in red wine and napped in a tantalizing sauce of mushrooms and pearl onions) and meltingly sinful scrambled eggs in flaky, buttery puff pastry.

*F*rench-style desserts range from the not-so-sweet assiette de fromage—thin wedges of cheese such as Brie or Maytag blue with a couple of perfect figs and apricots—to a very sweet flourless chocolate cake.

and Houston Sts.; **Kate's Paperie** at Broadway and Prince, for a wide range of extraordinary papers.

Barney Greengrass

541 AMSTERDAM AVENUE BET. 86TH AND
87TH STREETS
724-4707
SATURDAYS AND SUNDAYS, 8:30 A.M.—5 P.M.
RESERVATIONS NOT ACCEPTED.
$$
CASH ONLY

You know right off that you haven't come for the decor. It's a dingy place with peeling wallpaper, deli cases up front, and sawdust sprinkled liberally on the floor. But step in and feast on some of the finest smoked sturgeon, nova, and whitefish that New York can dish out. Barney Greengrass, after all, is the city's self-proclaimed Sturgeon King.

The fish is superb—moist, delicately flavored, and, importantly, it's perfectly sliced. You'd trust these countermen to perform brain surgery. There is beautiful smoked salmon, of course, but also sable (smoked cod flavored with garlic and paprika), herring in various cream- and vinegar-based sauces, salty lox, as well as whitefish and tuna salads. Order anything. It's all great. But notice: The regulars always get at least one order of Greengrass's

In the Neighborhood

The **Museum of Natural History** and the **Rose Center for Earth and Space** at Central Park West and 79th St.; **New York Historical Society** at Central Park West and 77th St.; **Summit Rock**, the highest elevation in Central Park bet. 81st and 85th. Sts.

renowned nova, eggs, and onions. The onions are caramelized and swirled with scrambled eggs and chunks of nova. Team it with a smoked fish appetizer, a healthy portion of fish, tomatoes, onion, and cream cheese. You can request more bagels should you run out.

*M*ust have meat? You can't lose. Savor the pastrami and corned beef—you're not likely to have it this good for a while. Order it on soft, chewy rye or cooked into scrambled eggs.

*S*hould you have room for dessert, order a hunk of chocolate babka or a few rugalach to dunk in your coffee. Then pay your check to Moe Greengrass, who sits regally behind the cash register. If you're a kid, or one at heart, he'll give you a lollipop.

Blue Water Grill

31 UNION SQUARE WEST AT 16TH STREET
675-9500
SUNDAYS, 11 A.M.—4 P.M.
RESERVATIONS ACCEPTED.
$$
AMEX, V, MC

*I*f seafood is your passion, brunch at the Blue Water Grill is a must. The signature dish is oysters, served on the half shell or crisply fried with poached eggs, corn fritters, and Cajun hollandaise. There are lobsters, clams, crabs, and smoked salmon, too, all reliably fresh and wonderfully prepared. Beyond seafood, other brunch items include an assortment of omelets, a roast chicken salad with goat cheese and basil-pesto vinaigrette, and a burger with fries.

*W*hatever you choose, you'll enjoy the setting: a former bank with grandly soaring ceilings, gleaming white marble, and shining brass. In warm weather, you can dine alfresco at tables under the awning along 16th Street. The Union Square clientele—a typical mix of young couples, families and students—gathers to listen to the jazz trio that plays in a corner by the

In the Neighborhood

Union Square Park; on Saturday, the **Union Square Greenmarket** on the northern and western perimeters of the park; **Paragon Sport** for equipment and clothing and **ABC** for home furnishings, both on Broadway at 18th St.; **Strand Bookstore** at Broadway ➤

15

copper bar on Sundays. Owner Stephen Hanson, the man behind Isabella's, Ocean Grill, and Park Avalon, has created a sophisticated yet accessible restaurant with a friendly wait staff who seem to be able to serve a full house without a hiccup.

and 12th St. for a great selection of used and hard-to-find titles.

Cafe con Leche

424 AMSTERDAM AVENUE BET. 80TH AND 81ST STREETS
726 AMSTERDAM AVENUE BET. 95TH AND 96TH STREETS
595-7000, 678-8000
SATURDAYS AND SUNDAYS, 10 A.M.—4 P.M.
RESERVATIONS NOT ACCEPTED.
$
AMEX, V, MC

One sip of this restaurant's namesake beverage, a creamy, potent cafe con leche, evokes its Caribbean roots. It offers the best Cuban-Dominican brunch in the city. In both locations, the narrow, casual urban/tropical spaces are slick and sunny, with brilliant aqua-and-blue tables. Walls covered with quilted aluminum and cheery yellow wainscoting are enlivened with colorful masks and bold oil paintings. Salsa and rumba rhythms on the sound system overwhelm the noise of the whirring blender that's in constant use behind the long counter.

*T*he menu features classic, high-calorie, Latin-style fare, such as sweetened plantains, rice and beans, and batidos (an extra-creamy, fruit-filled milk shake without ice cream). But you can also get tostada francesa (French toast), omelets with chorizo (spicy Spanish sausage), and fried eggs, jazzed up with hefty portions of pernil asado (roast pork). There's biftec a la parilla (a lean steak), too, and the equally appealing Cuban sandwich, piled high with ham, roast pork, and pickles; rice topped with spicy black beans and vegetables; and the hearty ropa vieja (shredded beef). Order a side of mofongo (mashed green plantains peppered with pork rinds). Olé!

In the Neighborhood

At Broadway and 96th St., the epicurean paradise called the **Gourmet Garage**; stroll southward through **Riverside Park** to the **79th Street Boat Basin**, where houseboats bob away on the Hudson.

Cafe des Artistes

1 West 67th Street at Central Park West
877-3500
Saturdays, 11 A.M.-2:45 P.M.;
Sundays, 10 A.M.-2:45 P.M.
Reservations suggested.
$$$$
AmEx, V, MC

The romantic atmosphere at Cafe des Artistes is owed largely to the sensuous Depression-era murals of pert naked ladies by illustrator Howard Chandler Christy (of "Christy girl" fame) that are found throughout the room. Owner George Lang encourages weekly menu changes at the whim of Austrian chef Thomas Ferlesch, but the restaurant's famous popovers are always available, served with little pots of strawberry butter and jam. And you can expect scrambled eggs plated over thin slices of fresh brioche, with dill-infused gravlax; impossibly tender meat in the succulent pot-au-feu with bone marrow; and pungent bourride (fish stew) with aioli. The weekly inspirations might include a vegetarian platter served "in the Middle Eastern manner" with pita bread; or crisply sauteed soft-shell crabs; or a salad of vine-ripe tomatoes with snow white anchovies, basil, and onions.

In the Neighborhood

Tour **Lincoln Center's theaters** or sit in its park, linger by the "dancing" fountain and the reflecting pool, and see the Chagalls in the windows of the **Met**; **Maya Schaper Cheese and Antiques** on 69th St. bet. Columbus Ave. and Broadway for a perfect little silver salt cellar, or the very best oozing Brie.

*Y*ou'll be tempted and delighted by the novel dessert, Mr. Christy's ice cream palette, a colorful assortment of ice creams and sorbets—in flavors like black currant and cheesecake—arranged like daubs of paint on an artist's palette, and served with tiny ramekins of hot fudge and strawberry coulis. And have a cup of tea; it comes in charming little double pots.

Cafe Gitane

242 MOTT STREET AT PRINCE STREET
334-9552
SATURDAYS AND SUNDAYS, 9 A.M.—11:30 P.M.
RESERVATIONS NOT ACCEPTED.
$
CASH ONLY

*R*estaurateur Luc Levy has created a hip cafe setting on a peaceful NoLita (north of Little Italy) block. During his summer "film festival," movies are projected on the church wall across the street.

*A*t Cafe Gitane, you can sit undisturbed with a cup of coffee or perhaps tea made with fresh mint leaves and read a magazine plucked from the rack next to your table. Levy manages to prepare all of his tasty food in a narrow prep kitchen behind the bar. His specialties include smoked salmon tartare with red onions, capers, and lemon wasabi mayonnaise on a toasted sourdough baguette; Moroccan couscous with zesty chicken, red peppers, pine nuts, eggplant, and hummus; and a wonderfully light dish of plump dates served with shaved Parmesan atop crusty peasant bread.

*T*he brunch menu is served at all hours and includes a selection of croissants, homemade granola with fruit and yogurt, and eggs baked with basil, tomato, and cream. If you are dining alone and prefer the coziness of the bar, there is usually a stool open with enough elbowroom for your own copy of Le Monde.

In the Neighborhood

NoLita (North of Little Italy), a burgeoning downtown area worth a browse for its Left Bank ambience and new cutting-edge boutiques; for shoes, **Sigerson-Morrison** on Mott St., between Houston and Prince; and for used designer women's clothes in excellent condition, stop at **Ina** on Thompson St.

Cafe M

STANHOPE HOTEL, 995 FIFTH AVENUE BET.
80TH AND 81ST STREETS
717-0303
SATURDAYS AND SUNDAYS,
NOON—4 P.M.
RESERVATIONS
ACCEPTED.
$$$
AMEX, V, MC

Optimally situated for people-watching, Cafe M is directly across the street from the Metropolitan Museum of Art, with all of its hustle and bustle. Take a seat at one of the colorful bistro chairs under the candy-striped awning, order a Bloody Mary, and kick back to watch the goings-on. Vendors sell black-and-white photos of the city, a musician plays his violin, and a busload of European schoolchildren, all toting colorful backpacks, scampers about noisily. Sitting around you is a mix of camera-toting out-of-towners, society matrons decked in Chanel, and culture vultures brunching before or after a visit to the museum. Of course, you may opt to dine inside in the elegant dining room, where the art on the walls looks, oddly enough, like lipstick smears; but it's the outdoor space that sets this restaurant apart.

*H*appily, the food is as inspired as the setting. Matthew Kenney, one of Manhattan's most creative chefs, has developed a varied and imaginative menu that includes brunch items, salads, raw bar selections, and heartier fare for the late-afternoon crowd. Strict brunch fans should opt for the perfectly fried eggs with spicy duck sausage, the   cinnamon French toast, or the tomato omelet loaded with zucchini and chive blossoms. The adventurous, however, might begin with the sumptuous plateau de fruits de mer for two before moving on to charcoaled lamb chops with Provençal tomatoes; the perfect-for-fall rabbit stew with chanterelles, spring vegetables, and Riesling; or the comfort-with-a-twist macaroni with a walnut herb-pesto.

In the Neighborhood

The **Metropolitan Museum of Art**, directly across the street, for the art or the shops; walk up **Museum Mile** for the **Guggenheim, Cooper-Hewitt, Jewish Museum,** and **International Center of Photography**.

Cafeteria

119 SEVENTH AVENUE AT 17TH STREET
414-1717
SATURDAYS AND SUNDAYS, 6 A.M.—5 P.M.
RESERVATIONS SUGGESTED.
$
AmEx, V, MC

Don't let the name fool you; there are no molded gelatin salads or tuna surprise specials to be found at Cafeteria. White mod chairs, banquettes, terrazzo floor, a front wall of glass, garage doors that open to the sidewalk in warm weather, and waitresses in Dolce & Gabbana take this downtown diner way upscale.

The surprise is that the exceptional brunch and lunch fare is reasonably priced, and the sparse decor contrasts delightfully with the generous comfort food from chef Tyler Florence. His all-day brunch menu offers French toast, given a buttery spin with croissants and maple-flavored apples, and savory and satisfying smoked salmon and potato hash topped with poached

In the Neighborhood

Authentiques, 255 West 18th St. bet. Seventh and Eighth Aves., for glassware, lamps, bowls, memorabilia and Christmas ornaments;➤

23

eggs and a dollop of dill hollandaise.
There is juicy fried chicken, too—a
crispy treat with a side of buttermilk
waffles and sweet maple jus.

*C*lothing designer Victor Alfaro is
one of the owners, so it's not
surprising that the stylishly dressed
fashion crowd frequents this place.
You'll leave comfortably sated and
pleased with the bill.

Canal House

AT THE SOHO GRAND HOTEL
310 WEST BROADWAY BET. GRAND
AND CANAL STREETS
965-3588
SATURDAYS AND SUNDAYS, 11 A.M.—3 P.M.
RESERVATIONS SUGGESTED.
$$$
AMEX, V, MC

**Chisholm
Larsson
Gallery**, 145
Eighth Ave. at
17th St., for
WWI, WWII,
Polish, Swiss and
French posters;
**Housing
Works Thrift
Shop** on 17th
St. east of
Seventh Ave., a
stylish, bargain-
hunters mecca
where all pro-
ceeds go to a
worthy cause.

*T*he SoHo Grand's industrial-chic
lobby is furnished with comfy,
overstuffed gray sofas from which you
can watch the passing parade of
celebs. But proceed to the light-filled
dining room at the far end of the
lobby. Diaphanous curtains shade
floor-to-ceiling windows, fans turn
slowly overhead, and silver-leafed art

works grace the walls. And there's rarely a crowd, as Canal House is still something of an undiscovered gem. What we love best about it is the wonderfully surprising combination of brunch items. A bowl of golden fried-apple-and-corn beignets offers plenty for two to share. In a twist on the New Orleans classic, they come topped with powdered sugar, of course, but also with crispy bacon. Other favorites include asparagus, wild mushroom, and goat cheese-filled omelet, and a grilled bagel club—a tower of herbed cream cheese, smoked salmon, and grilled red onions piled atop a thinly sliced bagel and served with vegetable chips.

*I*t's easy to spend an entire morning at one of the cozy tables with a pile of newspapers and magazines. Be careful, though: You might discover that the day has come and gone.

In the Neighborhood

Dozens of art galleries including **Larry Gagosian**; boutiques like **Dolce & Gabbana** on West Broadway, and Wooster St. for **Todd Oldham**; **The Guggenheim SoHo** and the **New Museum of Contemporary Art** and, for cutting edge, socially conscious exhibitions, on Broadway bet. West Houston and Prince Sts.; **Angelika Film Center** on Houston at Mercer St. for a late-afternoon art house flick and a steaming cappuccino.

Capsouto Freres

451 WASHINGTON STREET AT WATTS STREET
966-4900
SATURDAYS AND SUNDAYS, NOON—3 P.M.
RESERVATIONS SUGGESTED.
$$$
AmEx, V, MC

Finding your way this far west can be a bit tricky, so hope that you'll be lucky enough to find Mrs. Capsouto (mother to brothers Albert, Jacques, and Samuel) at the table by the door and her artichoke ragout on the Specials menu.

Chef Eric Heinrich has created a Menu de Brunch that celebrates classic French dishes: soupe a l'oignon gratinée, rich with bread and cheese; beautifully layered terrine a la Provençal; buttery sole amandine; melt-in-your-mouth confit de canard; and classic steak frites. He offers eggs Benedict, too, and salade niçoise, and occasionally a warming cassoulet in the winter months. Chef Heinrich also spoils us with grapefruit and ginger-rhubarb jams to spread on fresh breads—and fig jam, too, in-season. Between courses, cleanse your palate the French way, with homemade

In the Neighborhood

TriBeCa Potters (call ahead: 431-7631) at Greenwich St. bet. Vestry and Desbrosses has the work of about 10 potters available for sale; **Olio**, on Greenwich and Watts, for original home furnishings; walk to **Battery Park** and the very tip of Manhattan along the ➤

sorbets in such flavors as Concord grape, Pinot Noir, pear, and raspberry. A delectable slice of tarte Tatin, the classic French pastry made of caramelized apples, is the perfect way to complete your meal.

*C*apsouto Freres occupies a TriBeCa landmark warehouse renovated by the brothers. With brick walls, an inviting terrace, climbing plants in the windows, and frosted-glass chandeliers, the dining room feels relaxed, yet elegant and as friendly as the Capsouto brothers- Jacque, Samuel, and Albert- who pause attentively at each table. If you are a devotee of French fare, come to Capsouto Freres. Bon appetit.

Hudson River promenade, and then take in the vista from **The Observatory** atop the **World Trade Center**.

The Comfort Diner

214 EAST 45TH STREET BET. SECOND AND
THIRD AVENUES
867-4555
SATURDAYS AND SUNDAYS, 9 A.M.—4 P.M.
RESERVATIONS NOT ACCEPTED.
$
AMEX, V, MC

When you are in the mood for diner food, but not the predictable coffee shop variety, head for The Comfort Diner with its zero attitude, New York clientele, and retro decor—complete with bowling trophy lamps and quilted aluminum wall and counter treatment.

Cloth napkins are the first clue that this is not your average greasy spoon. Yes, there are mustard pots at the table, and yes, there are rows of tiny cereal boxes stacked above the dessert case. But skip the Rice Krispies and scan the menu, where you'll find berry-stuffed French toast—two enormous slices of wonderfully fresh challah with deep pockets stuffed with blueberries that are so sweet and moist you'll find no need to reach for the syrup. Another brunch favorite is red flannel hash: poached eggs over a savory and sweet melange of potatoes, sweet potatoes, corned beef, and beets. The Brooklyn-born egg cream (gentrified with cappuccino) is good here, and made at your table with seltzer spritzed from a vintage cobalt-blue bottle. The chocolate dispenser is left for "topping off." Of the ultrasweet desserts on tap, none is sweeter than deep-dish pecan pie—ask for it warmed—or a slice of peanut-stuffed Snickers pie with homemade ice cream. But be sure to ask for an extra spoon, or two.

In the Neighborhood

The newly renovated **Grand Central Terminal**, one of New York's great landmarks, with its fabulous shops and famous restaurants, including **Michael Jordan's Steak House** and the **Oyster Bar**; walk over to the **United Nations**, First Ave. and 45th St., and view the East River from the **UN Garden**.

Copeland's

547 WEST 145TH STREET BET. AMSTERDAM
AVENUE AND BROADWAY
234-2357
SUNDAYS, NOON—2 P.M., 2 P.M.—4 P.M.
RESERVATIONS SUGGESTED.
$$$
AMEX, V, MC

A gospel brunch? Amen, you'll say to this Harlem establishment's copious Sunday "soul buffet," complete with gospel singers. If you arrive early for either of the two seatings, you can sit at the bar and enjoy a spicy Bloody Mary jazzed up with a dash of steak sauce. While waiting, you can also scope out the buffet that sits just beside the door and watch the servers fill platters with fried chicken, okra, and grits. At noon and 2 P.M. sharp, the doors open, but before patrons rush the buffet, the owner of Copeland's stands and offers grace.

*I*nstead of joining the herd, wait about 20 minutes for the line to thin out. Then at a leisurely pace you can load your plate with collard greens, spicy beef sausage, fried apples, hush puppies, even mussel-filled seafood Newburg.

In the Neighborhood

The architecturally distinguished row houses known as **"Striver's Row,"** on West 138th and 139th Sts., bet. 7th and 8th Aves., which have been home to famed African-American musicians, such as W.C. Handy and Eubie Blake; >

The gospel singers, who perform on a small stage, accompanied by a piano, tambourine, drums, and maracas provide the entertainment, but patrons sing along, too, clapping their hands and stomping their feet to tunes like "I'm Going to Let It Shine" and "Taking It to the Streets."

The Schomburg Center for Research in Black Culture on Lenox Ave. at 135th St.

After you have grooved for a while, pick yourself up for one last visit to the buffet table. The coconut cream pie is worth the trip.

Cub Room Cafe

183 PRINCE STREET AT SULLIVAN STREET
777-0030
SATURDAYS AND SUNDAYS, 11:30 A.M.—4 P.M.
RESERVATIONS NOT ACCEPTED.
$
AMEX, V, MC

Cub Room Cafe is a low-key, country-style oasis amidst the bustle of SoHo's shops and galleries. Food is served at farmhouse tables aglow with votive candles. Brick and wood-paneled walls are lined with bottles of flavored oils and colorful ceramic teapots.

Specials, as inviting as the surroundings, usually include homemade soup and sandwiches. We like the smoky black bean soup and the delicately flavored artichoke, arugula, and mozzarella sandwich on Tuscan bread. On the regular menu, a breakfast burrito is chock-full of fluffy scrambled eggs, black beans, roasted potatoes, and jack cheese and served with salsa verde and picante, guacamole, and sour cream. Eggs are made to order and served with miniature buttermilk biscuits, crunchy roasted potatoes, mesclun with a light vinaigrette, and

In the Neighborhood

SoHo's retail jungle: **Louis Vuitton, Tocca, Todd Oldham; Broadway Panhandler**, Broome St. at Wooster, for kitchenware and cake decorating supplies; **NoLita** shops for funky clothing and furniture and cozy cafes perfect for a late afternoon cafe au lait.

sausage or steak. The brioche French toast with Grand Marnier syrup is moist and pleasantly sweet, and the smoked salmon on a bagel is smoked in-house by the chef. The Cub Room's scrumptious pastries and cakes, baked fresh on the premises, might include bittersweet chocolate cake with espresso ice cream; warm apple crumble; or a selection of impossibly large and decadent cookies.

Danal

90 EAST 10TH STREET BET. THIRD AND
FOURTH AVENUES
982-6930
SATURDAYS AND SUNDAYS, 10 A.M.—3 P.M.
RESERVATIONS NOT ACCEPTED.
$
V, MC

Baskets of fruit and onions, potatoes and dried flowers are everywhere at this charmingly cluttered and bustling brunch spot. Twig wreaths and botanical plates adorn the yellow brick walls, and a weathered wheelbarrow (aged in the country, no doubt) evoke Martha Stewart, but with a downtown sense for the eclectic. There's a precious little garden, too, complete with piped-in bird chirping.

*C*hoose a candlelit farmhouse table or a Parisian-style marble-top for two, and peruse the framed menu. Among the many appealing seasonal choices can be croissant French toast with cinnamon and apples, or smoked salmon with delicate dill pancakes, and grilled shrimp on spinach, with a medley of avocado, cucumber, pine nuts, tomatoes, olives, and potatoes tossed in creamy blue-cheese dressing. Our particular favorite combo: onion soup and grilled chicken breast sandwich with tomato and Brie. In a nice, help-yourself-to-a-casual-weekend touch, coffee is served in individual Bodum French press coffeemakers at each table. Teas, brewed in squat, colorful pots, include a Provençal fruit infusion.

*D*anal's atmosphere is relaxed no matter how busy, but you can't make reservations, and you'll be seated only when your entire party arrives. The addition of a second floor has been a great improvement, but a bench outside and couches in the entryway are comfortable places to

In the Neighborhood

New York Central Art Supply, Third Ave. bet. 10th and 11th Sts., for rare papers; **Kiehl's** on Third Ave. and 13th St., a one-of-a-kind store for the natural beauty; **Astor Wines and Spirits**, a superb source for your wine cellar at Astor Place at Lafayette St.

perch should you have to wait for a table. You can feel at home here in jeans and a T-shirt or whatever you'd wear when you use your wheelbarrow.

Drovers Tap Room

9 JONES STREET BET. BLEECKER AND WEST 4TH STREETS
627-1233
SATURDAYS AND SUNDAYS, 11 A.M.—4 P.M.
RESERVATIONS SUGGESTED.
$$
AMEX, V, MC

Owners David Page and Barbara Shinn provide all-American comfort fare in an evocative Midwestern-style setting. Yellow-painted brick walls, wood floors, antique lamps

(from the city hall in Page's hometown of Berlin, Wisconsin), and a shiny red tin ceiling are offset by vintage snapshots of blushing brides and beaming race car drivers. A mason jar filled with fresh flowers sits atop each table.

*A*t Drovers, the crowd is a relaxed mix of young couples, grannies, and kids, who all come to while away the afternoon. Brunch usually starts with one of the refreshing house cocktails, like the brunch punch of freshly squeezed grapefruit juice paired with homemade lemon vodka. Bloody Mary fans in search of the perfect version will no doubt be extremely content with this one, fortified with fresh horseradish, black pepper, and pickled carrots.

*I*ron-skillet macaroni and cheese is topped with crispy, golden brown bread crumbs, Parmesan cheese,

and sliced cherry tomatoes. The Drovers grilled cheese sandwich comes with "overnight" tomatoes, country ham, and a side of home-style potato salad. And the burger satisfies the craving, with its aged Cheddar cheese and homemade ketchup. Another favorite is the Hangtown Fry: scrambled eggs with plump oysters, bacon, and plenty of spinach.

A spoonful of dense butterscotch pudding will kindle childhood memories.

In the Neighborhood

Pierre Deux, on the corner of Bleecker and Charles Sts. and other antiques stores along this famous stretch in the West Village, with its narrow, meandering, cobblestone streets and low-rise buildings.

E. A. T.

1064 MADISON AVENUE BET. 80TH AND
81ST STREETS
772-0022
SATURDAYS AND SUNDAYS, 7 A.M. ON.
RESERVATIONS NOT ACCEPTED.
$$$
AMEX ONLY

New Yorkers joke that E.A.T. is a Madison Avenue version of a classic Jewish deli with the most expensive breadbasket in town. Sure, it's pricey but after one bite of the dense, chewy raisin-flecked slices of baguettes slathered with raspberry jam and butter, you won't count the cost.

E.A.T.'s decor is slick and spare with black-and-white tiled floors, silver columns, and a giant, floor-to-ceiling window on Madison Avenue. The front deli counter is loaded with sumptuous salads and breads—all baked by Eli Zabar's Eli's Bread—of every size and shape. It's the perfect place to load up on goodies before heading, post-brunch, for the Hamptons.

The menu of simple, but beautifully prepared foods includes everything from standard deli fare—egg salad, meat loaf, and chopped liver sandwiches—to nouvelle and gourmet dishes. The salad plate allows you to choose three items from any of two dozen selections: beets, raw mushrooms with a grilled leek garnish, grilled vegetables, tabbouleh, and much, much more. Brunchers might opt for the omelet and salad, scrambled eggs loaded with salmon, smoked fish plate, or, for the ultimate in decadence, an omelet filled with Beluga caviar.

*W*orth every penny at a whopping $16, the dish we love best is macaroni and cheese—penne baked to a perfect crispiness with Asiago cheese, and paired with a mesclun salad.

In the Neighborhood

E.A.T. Gifts, next door, is a well-chosen selection of books, original gifts, and lots of kids stuff; the **Agnes b. boutique**; **Fresh**, which carries an amazing selection of skin care products; the **Metropolitan Museum**; the **Whitney Museum of American Art**.

Eighteenth and Eighth

159 EIGHTH AVENUE AT 18TH STREET
242-5000
SATURDAYS AND SUNDAYS, 9 A.M.—4 P.M.
RESERVATIONS NOT
ACCEPTED.
$$
AMEX, V, MC

A long line usually spills out onto Eighth Avenue at this ultra-Chelsea (read, very gay) brunch destination, where the wait staff and clientele are among the most attractive in town. Needless to say, the wait for the dozen-odd tables can be fierce.

Dried and fresh flowers, a collection of colorful teapots, and French doors that open onto the street in warm weather all contribute to the casual atmosphere. The affordable prix fixe—under $20—includes a choice of

In the Neighborhood

The **Joyce Theater**, on Eighth Ave. at 19th St., for modern dance; **The Dia Center for the Arts**, West 22nd St., with its permanent ➤

a Bloody Mary, mimosa, or orange juice, and the pages-long, diner-sized a la carte menu offers everything from three-egg omelets with a dozen fillings (including bananas!) to kiwi-orange and mango-raisin pancakes, organic buffalo burgers, and salads. A standout is the apple and sausage omelet, a terrific mix of sweet and savory, served with garlicky hash browns. A tasty, protein-packed energizing shake of spirulina, honey, yogurt, and bananas is a perfect finish.

collection of the works of Joseph Beuys, Cy Twombly, Andy Warhol, and others; Dia's cubicle-like roof sculpture by Dan Graham and the pocket-sized coffee bar for some mid-afternoon fortification.

Fifty-Seven Fifty-Seven

AT THE FOUR SEASONS HOTEL
57 EAST 57TH STREET BET. MADISON AND
PARK AVENUES
758-5757
SATURDAYS AND SUNDAYS, 11:30 A.M.—2 P.M.
RESERVATIONS SUGGESTED.
$$$$
AMEX, V, MC

Pale wood floors, pots of orchids, and agate-shaded lamps are but a few of the elegant touches that grace this posh hotel's dining room. The service is impeccable and the champagne cocktails are irresistible. The contemporary American menu has a dash of continental flair with a pinch of whimsy: the breadbasket, for instance, holds not only sesame-crusted flatbread but also glazed doughnuts from—surprise!—the ovens of Krispy Kreme. Among the outstanding dishes are natural goat's milk yogurt with berries, tender smoked trout and cucumber salad on a bed of baby mixed greens, and plump, lightly battered Maryland crab cakes with roasted bell-pepper aioli. An often requested item is the fragrant lemon ricotta hotcakes, topped with lemon zest, and served with applewood smoked bacon.

*F*ifty-Seven Fifty-Seven is a delight, and your every need will be anticipated.

In the Neighborhood

Prada, Coach, and **J.P. Todd's** on 57th St.; a few blocks north on Madison Ave., **Barneys New York, Armani,** and **Calvin Klein**; walk along **Park Ave.,** with its beautiful plantings in every season.

French Roast

2340 Broadway at 85th Street
799-1533
458 Sixth Avenue at 11th Street
533-2233
Saturdays and Sundays, 10 A.M.—4 P.M.
Reservations not accepted.
$
AmEx, V, MC

This duo of bistros—one on the Upper West Side and the other in the heart of the West Village—welcomes crowds around the clock, since they are open 24 hours. The mood is casual and breezy, and the setting quintessential French cafe, with its black-and-white tiled floors, mismatched chandeliers, marble-topped tables, and bistro chairs. Colorful antique signs decorate the walls and, in spring and summer, meals are served outside under jaunty red awnings. Prepare yourself for a bit of French attitude as well, and you'll feel right at home.

$\mathscr{A}$t the downtown location, the scene is funky and artsy. Men and women wearing retro eyeglasses gather with their leather-clad friends to discuss the latest gallery opening. Uptown, the crowd is all button-down shirts and khakis, sort of Gap with an edge. But at both locations you'll find plenty of kids in strollers, jumping up and down, and sipping tall glasses of orange juice and cups of hot chocolate beside their parents.

$\mathscr{T}$he menu includes most of the French standards: the croque monsieur is especially good, loaded with gooey Gruyere cheese and smoked ham. Omelets appear uncomplicated, garnished with crisp potatoes and watercress, but their simplicity belies the fillings, the likes of which are asparagus and Brie or roasted pepper, onion, and merguez sausage. For the health-conscious there is sesame-flecked granola topped with sliced strawberries, cantaloupe, pineapple, and a scoop of yogurt.

$\mathscr{A}$ caveat: The modelesque wait staff can be inattentive. You may have to wave several times for the check, but when it arrives, you'll realize that brunch here is a bargain, as none of the entrees is more than $10.

In the Neighborhood

Uptown: Riverside Park and **Central Park**; Riverside's charming **79th St. Boat Basin cafe** in summer.

Downtown: Balducci's food-as-art gourmet emporium on Sixth Ave. at 9th St.; continue on to **Washington Square Park**; take in an art film at the **Quad** on 13th St. bet. Fifth and Sixth Aves.; and a few doors beyond visit the original **Kate's Paperie**.

Good Enough to Eat

483 AMSTERDAM AVENUE BET. 83RD AND
84TH STREETS
496-0163
SATURDAYS AND SUNDAYS, 9 A.M.—4 P.M.
RESERVATIONS NOT ACCEPTED.
$
AMEX, V, MC

At Good Enough to Eat, dried flowers and sheaves of wheat spill from baskets, paintings of cows and pigs and a large quilt cover the walls, and a white-washed picket fence separates the small bar from the dining room. The feeling is pure country, and even the giant portions seem to have come straight from a farmer's kitchen. Favorites include hole-in-the-bread—two slices of whole wheat bread with grilled ham and eggs cooked in cutout centers; Vermont Cheddar and apple omelet; and cinnamon-swirl French toast.

*T*ake note: The giant pork sausages, which accompany many of the dishes, are the best in town. Equally popular is Irish oatmeal served with cinnamon-flecked toast and candy-bar inspired Peter Paul pancakes, liberally sprinkled with chocolate chips and coconut. If you're not up to a big country brunch, order one of the city-friendly cinnamon buns or scones from the glass case up front.

*T*he fresh-faced wait staff is attentive and the crowd is casual. Sarah McLachlan and k.d. lang croon over the sound system as you munch merrily away.

In the Neighborhood

The **Children's Museum of Manhattan**, on West 83rd St. between Broadway and Amsterdam Aves., includes exhibits dedicated to everything from Dr. Seuss to the world of water; the **Museum of Natural History** and its giant-screen **Imax Movie Theatre**.

The Grange Hall

50 COMMERCE STREET AT BARROW STREET
924-5246
SATURDAYS, 11 A.M.—2:45 P.M.;
SUNDAYS, 10:30 A.M.—3:45 P.M.
RESERVATIONS SUGGESTED, ESPECIALLY SUNDAY.
$
AMEX ONLY

Some of the West Village's most charming homes are located at this intersection, where Commerce curves gracefully to meet Barrow.

Known from the thirties until 1992 as the Blue Mill Tavern, the renamed Grange Hall has preserved most of the fixtures and design of the original with wooden booths and smoked glass sconces. A mural painted in WPA-style along the back wall depicts corn harvesters, and the butter-lemon walls complement the rich, curved wood of the mirrored bar.

The Grange Hall boasts down-home cooking at reasonable prices. You might start with a warm basket of banana-walnut or blueberry bread, then move on to Olivia's poached eggs with a creamy sauce of tarragon,

In the Neighborhood

The **Potted Garden florist** at Bedford St. between Sixth and Downing; **Chess Forum** at Thompson St. bet. West Third and Bleecker Sts. for a game with a chess wizard and a cup of post-brunch tea; for a retreat, visit **St. Luke's Garden** on Hudson St. bet. Barrow and ➤

thyme, and woodland mushrooms (the chef's old family recipe). Or wrap your mouth around grilled Virginia ham steak with eggs and fried cornmeal mush. All the frittata specials are good and among the sides not to be missed are lean chicken and apple sausage and Amish home fried potatoes with bacon. They come heaped on a plate, family-style.

Grove Sts.; it's like sitting in your own back-yard.

Jules

65 ST. MARK'S PLACE BET. FIRST AND
SECOND AVENUES
477-5560
SATURDAYS AND SUNDAYS, 11 A.M.—4 P.M.
RESERVATIONS ACCEPTED.
$
AMEX ONLY

Jules is as inviting at one in the morning as it is at 11 A.M. Walk down a couple of steps into this East Village hangout for one of the best and most reasonable bistro brunches in New York. You might be in a smoky Paris wine bar, what with the young international crowd sipping Bordeaux and the quartet of conga, flute, bass, and keyboard. There's an accordionist too, and an amusing assortment of souvenirs and posters along the side wall, like Chubby Checker's limbo records, and a large French flag.

𝒫atrons and musicians tend to gather here in the midafternoon. There are a few tables outside in fair weather. Inside, fresh flowers, well-worn red banquettes, and cast-iron columns add to the Gallic charm. Jules has a well-priced prix fixe menu with a choice of egg dishes served with potatoes and mesclun salad, or French toast and fresh fruit. The create-your-own omelet (try savory tomato confit and creamy goat cheese) is outstanding as are the poached eggs draped in translucent smoked salmon and sprinkled with red onion. A la carte items include some bistro standards like steak frites with green peppercorn sauce and onion soup—and the ham and Swiss croque monsieur topped with bechamel sauce is worth the indulgence. For a sweet end to brunch at Jules, order pot au chocolat—marvelously dense and rich with a texture somewhere between a mousse and a pudding.

In the Neighborhood

St. Mark's Place, one of the most interesting streets for punk people watching; **St. Mark's Bookshop**, Third Ave. at 9th St., with an unusually good selection of books; 9th St. bet. First and Second Aves., for a plethora of odd boutiques—like **Mostly Bali**, open after 1 P.M., for Indonesian carved wood and textiles.

Kang Suh

1250 BROADWAY AT 32ND STREET
564-6845
OPEN 24 HOURS.
RESERVATIONS NOT ACCEPTED.
$$$
AMEX, V, MC

The best unconventional brunch in town is grill-it-yourself barbecue at Kang Suh. Pass by the sushi bar and head up the stairs where regulars enjoy house specialties such as bul go gi gui (marinated prime sirloin), marinated shrimp gui, and dak gui (marinated boneless chicken).

Before the grilling starts, sample a few of Kang Suh's excellent appetizers: pa jun, a scallion red and green pepper pancake with dipping sauce; jab chae, rice noodles with mixed vegetables flavored with beef; or the mildly spiced gop dol bi bim bab—sliced zucchini, carrots, spinach and sprouts with beef over rice in a sizzling stone dish.

The arrival of aromatic wood coals deposited in the grill in the middle of your table is your cue to get ready to barbecue. While your beef, shrimp, or chicken grills for a minute or two, sample several small dishes such as spicy kimchi, preserved crab, and seaweed salad that have been brought to your table. The grilled meat is eaten on a broad lettuce leaf, dabbed with chili and bean paste, and sprinkled with scallions, chili slices, or garlic. Fingers are proper here, so wrap it up and revel in an inspired combination of flavors.

The brick walls, exhaust fans, and linoleum floors do not make for fancy surroundings, but the aroma of the Kang Suh barbecue will seduce your senses.

In the Neighborhood

Venture over to **26th St. and Sixth Ave.** and scope out the city's most famous **flea market** complete with antiques, trash and treasures, odds and ends, every Saturday and Sunday; or see what's new in the **Cellar at Macy's**, on 34th St. and Sixth Ave., the world's largest department store.

Kitchenette

80 WEST BROADWAY AT WARREN STREET
267-6740
SATURDAYS AND SUNDAYS, 9 A.M.—4 P.M.
RESERVATIONS NOT ACCEPTED.
$
AMEX ONLY

*E*njoy a country-store-style brunch in a funky, retro atmosphere at Kitchenette, where mismatched chairs, whitewashed wainscoting, ceiling fans, and pots of geraniums in the windows define the decor. Counter stools overlook the griddle, and a glass case is stocked with gargantuan, tempting baked goods. We always ask for a cupcake topped with flaky coconut frosting.

*T*he farmhouse breakfast—two eggs served with potatoes and a fluffy buttermilk biscuit—will fill you up for the day. Other winning choices include the hearty sweet-potato hash with two eggs, biscuit, and corn-tomato relish; spicy gingerbread waffles with pumpkin butter; and an omelet loaded with smoked turkey, red peppers, and Cheddar cheese. Finish with a slice of sour cream coffee cake or a selection from the fountain menu—a chocolate malt, perhaps, or a variation of the Creamsicle—vanilla ice cream and orange juice, served in a tall glass.

In the Neighborhood

Designer discounts at **Century 21**, where underwear, tights, and socks are a perennial deal, and there's always an enormous selection of cut-price clothing, and lingerie; walk along the **Hudson River** to **Battery Park**.

La Belle Epoque

827 BROADWAY, BET. 12TH
AND 13TH STREETS
254-6436
SATURDAYS, 11:30 A.M.—3:30 P.M.;
SUNDAYS, 12 P.M.—4 P.M.
RESERVATIONS ACCEPTED.
$$ (SAT.); $$$ (SUN. BUFFET)
AMEX, V, MC

The extravagant setting is an art nou-
veau ballroom where you can enjoy
a sumptuous French/Creole/American
buffet and jazz brunch-cum-swing-
dancing every Saturday and Sunday. The
location is one steep, walk-up flight (or
a short elevator ride) above owner
Howard Kaplan's landmark street-level
antiques emporium. Kaplan furnished
La Belle Epoque from his vast collection
of French antiques and reproductions,
including signs from the Paris metro
and Les Halles stained-glass peacock
behind the bar. With its sinuous
wrought-iron accents and frosted-glass
sconces, the space has wonderful natural acoustics and rocks to the vibrations
of a different band every week. (You'd
never guess the space was once used by
a tobacco company in the 1860s, and by
the painter Willem de Kooning as a
studio in the 1950s.)

The menu for the prix fixe buffet varies from week to week, but the omelet station where you select your own fillings is standard. You might find the unusual egg St. Charles—a poached egg on a piece of fried trout—or several vegetarian dishes, such as fettuccine with mixed vegetables, or an array of luncheon items in the French/Creole/American traditions—coq au vin or jambalaya, for example. Saturdays, the jazz brunch has an a la carte menu that might feature muffaletta—a loaf of bread stuffed and layered with Italian sandwich ingredients—a spicy seafood gumbo, or tender scrod sauteed with papaya beurre blanc. For dessert, there's a devilishly rich chocolate cake and, usually, caramel banana bread pudding.

In the Neighborhood

At Broadway and 12th St., **The Strand Bookstore**, a New York landmark that always features an eclectic mix of used and out-of-print titles; take in a film at the new **Union Square movie complex**, at Broadway and 13th St.,and recline in one of the most comfortable seats in town.

La Lunchonette

130 TENTH AVENUE AT 18TH STREET
675-0342
SATURDAYS AND SUNDAYS, 11:30 A.M.—6 P.M.
RESERVATIONS SUGGESTED.
$$
AMEX, V, MC

At the epicenter of the burgeoning West 20s art scene, La Lunchonette is the best spot to brunch pre- or post-gallery hopping on Saturday. (Most galleries are closed Sunday.) The Dia Center for the Arts, with its spectacular rooftop views, is nearby, as are at least a dozen galleries, including Matthew Marks and Barbara Gladstone.

Brunch here is like a trip to a cheery cafe in the Marais. The walls glow lacquer red and sunlight filters through lace-curtained windows. Rosemary and miniature orange grow in terra-cotta pots on the windowsills. On the sound system, a plaintive Piaf-like chanteuse sings of la tristesse and le bonheur. Hostess/co-owner Melva Max, wife of chef/co-owner Jean-

Francois Fraysse, greets guests with "Honey!" and welcomes regulars and newcomers with equal affection.

*A*s soon as you are seated, a basket of hearty peasant breads, made at the Sullivan Street Bakery, appears with pots of butter and strawberry-rhubarb jam. Small blackboard menus at each table announce the daily specials, which might include venison with foie gras and quince; a hearty cassoulet; or roast chestnut and cauliflower soup. The lobster bisque is an especially good starter, loaded with sweet meat in a creamy, pale pink broth. The brunch menu, which is served from late morning until dinnertime, also offers generously portioned omelets, salads, and sandwiches. We love the ham, onion, and Gruyere omelet accompanied by green beans and potatoes gratin.

*A*s for the brunch clientele, it's a fun, funky mix of Chelsea denizens, families with kids engrossed in Eloise, and couples immersed in art brochures gleaned from long afternoons spent wandering the galleries.

In the Neighborhood

The **art galleries of Chelsea**, including the not to be missed space at the **Paula Cooper Gallery** on West 21st St; **Comme des Garcons**, created in a former garage on 22nd St. bet. Tenth and Eleventh Aves.

Le Jardin Bistro

25 CLEVELAND PLACE BET. KENMARE AND
SPRING STREETS
343-9599
SATURDAYS AND SUNDAYS, NOON—3 P.M.
RESERVATIONS NOT ACCEPTED.
$
AMEX, V, MC

*S*itting under the grape arbor at Le Jardin Bistro, you might imagine yourself to be in the French country-side. The casual atmosphere in the brick-walled garden is enhanced by a collection of amusing frog statues—an indication of the jovial owner's sense of humor.

*T*he menu is short and the food is simply prepared and very good. Highlights include the house country paté, a rich soupe de poisson that comes with a garlicky rouille mayonnaise and croutons; and the omelet Lyonnaise, filled with tender potatoes and caramelized onions. The delicious salade niçoise is made with fresh tuna, and the oeufs poches royal, an eggs Benedict variation, comes with smoked salmon. The croque monsieur, extra-redolent of ham and cheese, is served with mesclun and long and crispy pommes frites. And that bistro

In the Neighborhood

Urban Archaeology, Lafayette St. bet. Prince and Houston, for lighting and bathroom fixtures, new and old; **The Small Furniture Co.,** Lafayette St. at Bond St., restores, repairs, and sells chairs, side tables, desks, and more, sometimes at nice prices; ➤

standard, steak frites, is tres bon.

*W*hatever your choice, you will be tempted to linger over cups of espresso late into the afternoon.

stop in at the **Open Center Meditation Room** on Spring bet. Broadway and Crosby St.

Le Madeleine

403 WEST 43RD STREET BET. NINTH AND
TENTH AVENUES
246-2993
SATURDAYS AND SUNDAYS, NOON—3 P.M.
RESERVATIONS SUGGESTED.
$$
AMEX, V, MC

*T*ucked away in the heart of the Theater District, this bistro harbors a surprise: a lushly planted, enclosed garden where a delightful brunch is served year-round. A giant ficus tree dominates the vaulted, glass-domed space, offering shade on sunny days. Ivy trails from terra-cotta pots shaped like classical heads that gaze from the walls, and a decorative fountain bubbles in the corner.

Recommended appetizers are the Basque-style steamed mussels in a garlicky broth, served in a giant bowl with chorizo sausage, and a large-enough-for-two salade Madeleine—a mix of endive, apples, and toasted walnuts topped with Roquefort croutons. Outstanding main dishes include eggs Florentine—poached eggs and sauteed spinach on an English muffin—and the Mediterranean grilled chicken salad with currant-flecked couscous and eggplant caponata. Here, a grilled hamburger receives an elegant dollop of bearnaise sauce and is served with mesclun and red-wine onion confit. The chunky tarte Tatin is served with a bowl of whipped cream.

In the Neighborhood

The **Theater District**, with many opportunities to see matinee performances; same-day discount tickets at the TKTS booth on Times Square; **Ninth Ave.'s topnotch markets** for cheese, vegetables, and Greek and Italian delicacies.

Lenox Room

1278 THIRD AVENUE BET. 73RD
AND 74TH STREETS
772-0404
SUNDAYS, NOON—2:30 P.M.
RESERVATIONS SUGGESTED.
$$$
AMEX, V, MC

*S*unday brunch at Lenox Room is subdued, civilized, and urbane. Soft jazz from the Paul Lindemeyer Trio emanates from the front of the house. Crushed ice glistens from within the glass-encased oyster bar on the balcony, and spotlighted flats of wheat grass flank the stairs, just beyond the monumental flower arrangements on either side of the wait station. With an informal yet elegant setting, executive chef Charlie Palmer (formerly of Aureole) and managing partner Tony Fortuna (previously manager/maitre d' of Lespinasse) have fathered a landmark in the shifting sea of the Upper East Side restaurant scene.

*N*ibble tiny, freshly baked muffins while you sip a Bellini (made with fresh peaches) or a fruit punch, but leave room for sweet cinnamon vanilla French toast with pineapple and banana. Yellowfin tuna tartare with

In the Neighborhood

The **Frick Collection** at 70th St. and Fifth Ave., or the collection of Asian Art at **Asia Society** at 70th St. and Park Ave.; the **Whitney Museum of American Art** at 75th St. and Madison Ave.

soy sauce, sesame oil, and toast points
is a refreshing option, and the classic
eggs Benedict rivals any in the city.

*T*he caramelized banana parfait has
great fifties appeal with rich
coconut and caramel sauce. Another
eye-catching dessert is the frozen
praline soufflé with bittersweet
chocolate sauce. If lemon fits your
fancy, try the lemon custard pie with
pineapple mango relish.

Les Deux Gamins

170 WAVERLY PLACE AT GROVE STREET
807-7357
SATURDAYS AND SUNDAYS, 8 A.M.—4 P.M.;
WEEKDAYS, 8 A.M.—NOON.
RESERVATIONS NOT ACCEPTED.
$
AMEX ONLY

*I*f you wake up longing for a good,
foamy cafe au lait with a properly
flaky croissant, you'll find exactly that
at Les Deux Gamins. This charming,
well-worn spot is actually one of five
Gamins that French-born owner Robert
Arbor has opened around the city, each

a small slice of the Left Bank. Come for the fragrant coffee, the Valhrona hot chocolate, and the simply divine oeuf Gamin—a poached egg atop a crisp potato pancake filled with chèvre on a bed of tangy ratatouille. Pain perdu (French toast), omelets, and regular menu dishes are also available at brunch. Order a plate of hot and crispy pommes frites, a juicy steak au poivre, or steamed mussels with Muscadet and saffron sauce. There is a big selection of salads, sandwiches, and fish—just about everything you'd crave in a French bistro. Smoking is permitted here, as the cafe has less than 35 seats—and you will find the back room particularly inviting for a smoke, amid picture postcards and mirrors.

In the Neighborhood

Bleecker St. with its crush of Village locals and visitors, is home to an eclectic mix of food, fashion, record, and quirky boutiques; stop at **Murray's** on Bleecker at Cornelia St., for one of the finest selections of cheeses in the city; bring home a round semolina bread from **Zito's**; visit **Cones** for, what else, an extraordinary ice cream cone.

Le Zoo

314 WEST 11TH STREET AT
GREENWICH STREET
620-0393
SUNDAYS 11 A.M.—4 P.M.
RESERVATIONS NOT ACCEPTED.
$
CASH ONLY

*L*e Zoo is a perfect little neighbor-hood bistro offering one of New York's best values in brunches. Hang your coat on a hook as you walk in and treat it like the relaxed, friendly spot that it is. The sunny brick-walled dining room is decorated with French posters and dried flowers in flasks. You can sit at blue banquettes or on light wood chairs drawn up to small, white-cloth-covered tables.

*B*egin brunch with a mimosa, orange juice, or wine. The delectable main courses include meltingly tender duck confit salad with dried cherries, pears, pistachios, and sherry vinaigrette; poached eggs with home-made biscuits, chicken-apple sausage, and hollandaise; and a cream cheese and scallion omelet that you can count on to be fluffy. Have the vanilla-raisin bread pudding to finish, or, to satisfy your sweet tooth, classic crème brûlée.

In the Neighborhood

Bleecker St. shops—small clothing and gift boutiques, from **Emile Henri** to **Indonesian imports; Susan Parrish Antiques** at Bleecker bet. Perry and West 11th Sts. for great American quilts, folk art, and charming painted furniture.

*B*efore leaving, peek into the kitchen full of shiny stainless steel pots. With a competent staff that is and a reasonable menu that is always up to par, Le Zoo is a bright spot on the brunch scene.

Lola

30 WEST 22ND STREET BET. FIFTH
AND SIXTH AVENUES
675-6700
SATURDAY, SEATING AT 11:30 A.M.;
SUNDAYS, SEATINGS AT 9:30 A.M.,
11:30 A.M. AND 1:45 P.M.
RESERVATIONS STRONGLY SUGGESTED.
$$$$
AMEX, V, MC

*F*or the best gospel brunch south of 145th Street, where Copeland's reigns, head to the Flatiron District. For about a decade, Lola has been attracting gospel enthusiasts from all over the globe, but be forewarned: it's noisy, and gospel rhythms have patrons leaping to their feet between bites. But this gospel brunch has soul, and it's hopping on Sundays, when there's a line out the door, unless you make it to the 9:30 seating. All the performers are the real thing, but we are partial to Soul Resurrection, a group of seven singers and their band who perform every other Sunday. Their voices are as smooth and as satisfying as your first bite of Lola's banana-walnut bread.

*T*he large apricot-toned dining room easily seats 350 to 400 people. Large bamboo arrangements in terra-cotta vases divide the room that is lit by contemporary sconces and furnished with banquettes. But don't plan on remaining in your seat. You'll be encouraged to leap up and belt out "Oh Happy Day" along with the singers.

In the Neighborhood

Chelsea Billiards on 21st St. bet. Fifth and Sixth Aves.; walk Sixth Ave. bet. 18th and 23rd Sts. for popular shopping destinations such as **Filene's Basement, Bed Bath and Beyond, >**

$\mathcal{N}$ot to be missed is Lola's fried chicken, served with plantain chips on a bed of rice and Cuban-style baked beans with a lightly spiced crème fraîche. Other brunch offerings include caramelized banana challah French toast or an open-faced omelet with wilted spinach, plump capers, translucent red onions, and creamy feta. For dessert, included in the prix fixe, the chocolate truffle cake wins our vote, hands down.

TJ Maxx, Old Navy, and **Barnes and Noble** bookstore.

$\mathcal{A}$nd why not indulge? With all the foot-stomping and hand-clapping you've done, you've had your workout. And even if you're not spiritually inclined, swing by Lola on a Sunday and the spirit may just move you.

Mesa Grill

102 FIFTH AVENUE BET. 15TH
AND 16TH STREETS
807-7400
SATURDAYS AND SUNDAYS, 11:30 A.M.—3 P.M.
RESERVATIONS SUGGESTED.
$$$
AMEX, V, MC

esa Grill is a natural for brunch. If the funky bright lime-and-yellow color scheme doesn't wake you up, the spicy chicken and sweet potato hash topped with poached eggs and green chili hollandaise will. Mesa's menu presents the creative, boldly flavored, chili-based cuisine of superstar chef Bobby Flay (of cookbook and Food Network fame). It is complemented by an impressive list of tequilas to choose from. Try a pink cactus-pear margarita made with Heradura Silver.

Flay's Southwestern flare is evident in dishes like his white corn-crusted chile relleno, which is a hot and sweet medley of chiles stuffed with roasted beets and goat cheese, all served with grilled vegetables. The tuna tostada is grilled rare and served with a tangy black-bean mango salsa, and the chili pork sausage has a delicate apple-

In the Neighborhood

Lower Fifth Avenue shopping mecca from 14th to 23rd Sts., with **Emporio Armani, Joan and David, Banana Republic, Eileen Fisher; The Flatiron Building** (at 23rd St.); **Union Square Park** (bet. Broadway and Park Ave. and between 14th and 17th Sts.)➤

wood-smoked flavor. The house-ground hominy grits have a great, chewy texture and are sprinkled with fresh green onions. For a sweeter entree, try the toasted blue-corn pancakes served with bananas and fragrant orange-honey butter.

with its green-market filled with seasonal produce, flowers and baked goods, open Saturdays until about 5 P.M.; **Barnes and Noble** bookstore.

Mi Cocina

57 JANE STREET AT HUDSON STREET
627-8273
SUNDAYS, 11:30 A.M.—2:45 P.M.
RESERVATIONS ACCEPTED.
$
AMEX, V, MC

Mi Cocina offers authentic Mexican (not Tex-Mex) food in a tiny, brightly furnished restaurant. You will eat from rustic ceramic plates, sit at tables and chairs carved and painted in sun patterns, and relax in the warm glow of lemon yellow walls and terra-cotta floors.

The menu, which offers the city's best Mexican brunch, features a selection of refreshing beverages: fresh carrot juice flavored with a hint of lime, celery, or ginger; delicia de la mañana, a blend of strawberry, orange, peach, and banana fruit and juices; and margaritas, of course, that come in heavy-stemmed Mexican glasses.

The prix fixe includes your choice of fresh juice, entree, and coffee or tea, and each dish is meticulously prepared. The banana pancakes are stacked high and fluffy, served with banana slices and a pot of rich, homemade, caramelized goat's milk. Delicious egg dishes include an omelet spiced with fresh pico de gallo, serrano chile, and oozing with Mexican queso blanco; poached eggs with roasted tomato sauce, mildly spicy and tender poblano chile strips, and queso blanco, served with refried beans and tortillas. For something truly satisfying (and filling), try the huevos rancheros: two fried eggs on a corn tortilla with piquant salsa ranchera, served with refried beans and zucchini casserole. For aficionados of Mexican food, there is menudo, a tripe and hominy soup that is traditionally served there on Sundays.

The a la carte menu offers luncheon-type dishes, such as sauteed shrimp with spicy adobo sauce on a bed of steamed spinach, and grilled

In the Neighborhood

Mxyplyzyk, Greenwich Ave. at 13th St., for slick, modern design, small items for the home, lighting, tables, and some watches and stationery; across Greenwich Ave. bet. Jane and West 12th Sts., **Carry On Tea and Sympathy** for British goods, from Vegemite to tea cozies.

chicken breast with roasted poblano chiles and onions in a light cream sauce with crispy potatoes. For the kids, scrambled eggs, tacos, quesadillas, and pancakes are always available.

A word of caution here—if the waiter tells you it's spicy, he means it.

Odeon

145 West Broadway at Thomas Street
233-0507
Saturdays and Sundays, 11:30 a.m.—4 p.m.
Reservations suggested.
$$
AmEx, V, MC

*A*n Odeon brunch is a quintessential Manhattan experience. Glam supermodels huddle in banquettes, Hollywood types bark into cell phones, and jazz plays softly on the sound track, all while a capacity crowd schmoozes over the restaurant's excellent, inexpensive brasserie fare. Specials usually include smoked trout salad loaded with asparagus, radish, and endive, and butternut squash soup served with a rich dollop of crème fraîche. Among the favorites are French toast with apples and cinnamon, and eggs Hussard—poached eggs with grilled tomato and ham on an English muffin. The corned beef hash is topped, predictably, with poached eggs, but is served, surprisingly, alongside roasted beet salad with endive and walnuts. For diehards, there's a knockout cheeseburger with fries.

In the Neighborhood

The Screening Room, for a postprandial flick; shopping at **Century 21**; strolling along the **Hudson River promenade** to **Battery Park**.

Petite Abeille

400 WEST 14TH STREET AT NINTH AVENUE
727-1505
SATURDAYS AND SUNDAYS, 9 A.M.—5 P.M.
RESERVATIONS NOT ACCEPTED.
$
CASH ONLY

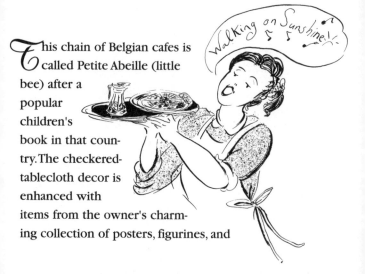

This chain of Belgian cafes is called Petite Abeille (little bee) after a popular children's book in that country. The checkered-tablecloth decor is enhanced with items from the owner's charming collection of posters, figurines, and books related to the comic character Tin Tin. At the Chelsea branch (107 West 18th Street), children's books are scattered about, available for kids to read.

*O*f the three Petite Abeille locations, we prefer this one, on far west 14th Street because there's less of a wait here, and because the ambience is especially nice. Pale lemon walls set off a colorful mural of Tin Tin and his pals and sprightly pop music, like Katrina and the Waves, spills from the open kitchen. As for the crowd, it's an interesting mix of uptowners, club kids, gallery-goers, and soccer moms. The brunch menu is tasty and inexpensive, ranging from salads and waffles to heartier "plats principaux." A favorite selection is the Omelette Maison, which is filled with a mix of smoked salmon, sour cream, and scallions. Other popular choices include waffles topped with fresh berries, salade niçoise, and, for a real meal, the medaillons de lotte, a monkfish filet with leeks and saffron.

In the Neighborhood

Chelsea Market on Ninth Ave. and 15th St., to stock up on everything from fresh-baked breads to meats, Thai seasonings, and potted plants; early morning in the **Meatpacking District**, dressed-to-kill transvestites, mustachioed men in leather chaps, and drag queens in feathered boas.

Petrossian

182 West 58th Street at Seventh Avenue
245-2214
Saturdays and Sundays, 11:30 a.m.—3 p.m.
Reservations suggested.
$$$$
AmEx, V, MC

Petrossian is opulence, glamour, and, most of all, caviar! This may be the only luxury restaurant in New York with a take-out counter right up front, where, on any given day, well-heeled shoppers order smoked fish, sumptuous portions of exotic caviars, and French pastries to go. In the art deco dining room, dapper waiters scurry about replenishing crystal champagne flutes with vintage bruts as sophisticated patrons ooh and aah over plates of scrambled eggs topped with glassy salmon roe or Sevruga caviar.

The Franco-Russian cuisine includes a light and flavorful borscht loaded with diced beets and accompanied by a pot of crème fraîche and a plate of miniature pierogis. Smoked river-trout salad with pickled beets and capers is served on a bed of mâche. The brioche French toast is

In the Neighborhood

Carnegie Hall for concerts; **The Museum of Modern Art** (MoMA) at 53rd St. bet. Fifth and Sixth Aves., for art, relaxing in the sculpture garden, a movie (tickets are free with the price of admission to the museum), or shopping at the two museum shops, for books and prints, or for beautifully designed objects and ➤

73

sprinkled with caramelized pecans. But the ultimate feast at Petrossian is the decadent dish of pressed caviar, smoked cod roe, and Russian salmon roe with blini and crème fraîche. Wow!

*Y*ou might expect such richesse to break the bank. Not so: The prix fixe menu, a selection of three courses, tops out at a reasonable $25. Watch for the refills of champagne, however, which can easily add up and send your bill skyrocketing.

housewares; across the street, **the American Craft Museum**; ten blocks downtown at 50th St. and Sixth Ave., **Radio City Music Hall**.

Popover Cafe

551 AMSTERDAM AVENUE BET. 86TH AND 87TH STREETS
595-8555
SATURDAYS AND SUNDAYS, 9 A.M.—3 P.M.
RESERVATIONS NOT ACCEPTED.
$$
AMEX, V, MC

*W*hat attracts brunchers in such droves? It's the namesake giant popovers, which are extra-fluffy and eggy on the inside and crispy on the outside, served with pots of ultra-decadent strawberry butter.

$\mathcal{H}$ave a seat at your cozy plaid-printed banquette amidst an assortment of teddy bears of all shapes and sizes. Honey bears on each table add a homey touch.

$\mathcal{B}$runch selections range from Irish oatmeal topped with warm apple sauce and brown sugar to lemon-twist pancakes with berries and lemon syrup. Omelets—with goat cheese, roasted red pepper, and fontina cheese—are especially popular, as are popovers stuffed with eggs, spinach, and Norwegian salmon. The regular menu includes salads, burgers, and hearty sandwiches.

In the Neighborhood

Popover's Plums, a country "emporium" piled high with pillows, crockery, and teddy bears, for a box of popovers and apple butter to be sent to friends at home.

75

Quilty's

177 PRINCE STREET BET. SULLIVAN AND
THOMPSON STREETS
254-1260
SATURDAYS AND SUNDAYS, 11:30AM—3PM.
RESERVATIONS ACCEPTED.
$$$
AMEX, V, MC

In 1998, Katy Sparks was named one of the ten best chefs of the year by Food & Wine magazine. So it's no wonder that her restaurant bustles at dinnertime. At brunch, however, the pace is leisurely, offering the perfect opportunity to sample chef Sparks's simple, beautifully prepared and presented contemporary American dishes.

Peach—yes, peach—beignets are spiced with cardamom sugar; red flannel salmon hash is topped with spinach and poached eggs; shirred eggs are baked in a casserole dish with thinly sliced Yukon Gold potatoes and spinach and sprinkled with fragrant herbs; and brioche French toast is garnished with peaches and mascarpone. The inspired menu also offers buttermilk-poppyseed pancakes, a flame-grilled cheeseburger with Vermont Cheddar, and a simple roasted

In the Neighborhood

Soho shopping; **Untitled** on Prince St. near Thompson St. for a cache of great postcards; Thompson St. for designers from **Betsey Johnson** to **Kate Spade.**

beet salad with haricots verts, aged
goat cheese, and walnuts.

*E*ven the decor is sublime at
Quilty's, soothing and elegant, with
pale lemon walls, polished dark wood
floors, and butterflies mounted in glass
frames. Jazz plays on the sound system, as you sip a drink and experience
brunch at its best.

Restaurant Florent

69 GANSEVOORT STREET BET. GREENWICH AND
WASHINGTON STREETS
989-5779
SATURDAYS AND SUNDAYS,
11 A.M.—4 P.M.
RESERVATIONS NOT ACCEPTED.
$
NO CREDIT CARDS

*F*lorent might look
like an average
New York quilted
aluminum diner,
but when you take in the
wait staff you quickly realize this place has an edge.
If you're lucky, charming
owner Florent may appear

dressed a la Marie Antoinette, as is his custom for the annual Bastille Day festivities.

*T*he not-just-brunch menu is, with a few exceptions, delightfully French, offering up, among other Gallic specialties, homemade rillettes, a rich potted paté made here with rosemary, boudin noir, and soppressata. There is also a homemade vegetable hash topped with poached eggs.

*T*he prix fixe brunch offers a choice of cocktail, coffee or tea, and main course for under $15. You can choose from dishes such as eggs Florentine, a goat cheese omelet with apples and onions, and vegetarian chili loaded with onion, tomato, and Cheddar cheese. But there's McCann's Irish oatmeal, too, and eggs with crispy french fries.

*T*he tables are tight, just like in your favorite Paris bistro, but that only makes for better eavesdropping for some good downtown dirt in this cool locale.

In the Neighborhood

Among the zillions of new **art galleries** opening in the meatpacking district, don't miss **Gavin Brown's Enterprise**, one of the hippest in town, on West 15th St bet. Ninth and Tenth Aves.

The River Cafe

1 WATER STREET AT THE BROOKLYN BRIDGE
718-522-5200
SATURDAYS, NOON—2:30 P.M.;
SUNDAYS, 11:30 A.M.—2:30 P.M.
RESERVATIONS SUGGESTED.
$$$$
AMEX, V, MC

*T*ake in spectacular views of the Big Apple from the elegant River Cafe, felicitously situated just under the Brooklyn Bridge. As you enjoy your brunch, you can see the Statue of Liberty downriver to your left, the Woolworth building and the spires of Wall Street at the southern tip of Manhattan, and the graceful span of the bridge overhead. Many customers drink in the view with a cocktail before ordering. The extensive wine list includes half-bottle selections of Veuve Clicquot demi-sec, and Taittinger. The bread and pastry basket is a marvelous assortment of goodies baked on the premises: corn sticks, mini banana muffins, raisin brioche, and almond croissants.

*T*he River Cafe is known for beautifully presented New American food. The smoked salmon appetizer appears with slices gently folded into a five-point star with a dollop of salmon mousse at the center and a smattering of salmon roe and diced red pepper— all served atop crisp-edged white corn crêpes and fines herbes. The salmon is smoked over fruitwood in the restaurant's smokehouse. The white asparagus and marinated beet salad is arranged in a pinwheel of colors and textures, with a three-minute egg at the hub. Entrees include poached Maine lobster, roast Amish farm chicken, and an omelet with grilled oysters. The sweet French toast of thick-sliced marbled brioche sits on a bed of salty country ham with berries. And the orange crêpes are made wonderfully tart and sweet by sides of warm, star ruby grapefruit, and a compote of fresh red currants and toasted almonds.

*C*ome to The River Cafe for a special occasion or a romantic interlude; you'll find the food rivals the view.

In the Neighborhood

The pedestrian walkway of the **Brooklyn Bridge**, a beautiful way to return to Manhattan; or, in summer, visit **The Anchorage** (inside the base of the great bridge) for art and music events in a cool, cavernous space.

Sarabeth's at the Whitney

WHITNEY MUSEUM
945 MADISON AVENUE AT 75TH STREET
570-3670
SATURDAYS AND SUNDAYS, 10 A.M.—4 P.M.
RESERVATIONS SUGGESTED.
$$
AMEX, V, MC

Where else in the city—or even the world—can you brunch surrounded by masterpieces of 20th-century art? At Sarabeth's at the Whitney, works by Franz Kline, Edward Hopper, Alexander Calder, and others beguile the eye as you dine.

We prefer this to the several other Sarabeth's locations for several reasons: the wait for tables is short if you arrive before noon, the tables are well spaced, and the service is exceptionally friendly.

Start off with a glass of the curiously named 4 Flowers juice, a deep-orange mix of banana, pineapple, orange, and pomegranate nectars. Standouts on the menu include the

In the Neighborhood

The **Whitney**, obviously, with its incomparable collection of 20th-century American art, including Georgia O'Keeffe's White Calico Flowers, Jasper Johns's Three Flags, and Edward Hopper's Early Sunday Morning.

goldie lox—scrambled eggs filled with smoked salmon and cream cheese— and the county-style pumpkin waffles topped with sour cream, pumpkin seeds, raisins, and honey. Other winning choices include the colorful frittata filled with red peppers, bacon, and Gruyere or the open-faced omelet with leeks, arugula, potatoes, and jack cheese.

Show up early at Sarabeth's—the museum doesn't open till 11 A.M.— and you'll have at least an hour before the crowds of guidebook-toting tourists descend on the place.

The Screening Room

**54 Varick Street bet. Canal and
Laight Streets**
334-2100
Sundays, 11:30 a.m.—3 p.m.
Reservations suggested.
$$$
AmEx, V, MC

*M*ovies are a feature of the week-
end menu at The Screening
Room, a restaurant where brunch can
be a knockout, all-day event. After
enjoying chef Mark Spangenthal's
inspired comfort foods and trendy
dishes, you can immerse yourself in
one of two movies: the enchanting
Breakfast at Tiffany's with Audrey
Hepburn, or the Jacqueline Susann
booze-and-pills camp classic, Valley of
the Dolls. They play on alternate days,
so call ahead to see if the movie suits
your mood.

*T*he dining room decor is an
homage to movie culture, with its
tufted, arched ceiling, maroon velvet
curtains and backlit photos of the
great New York movie palaces of
yore—the Capitol, the Lyric, and the
Paramount. A glowing red "L-I-Q-U-O-R"

sign, which hangs above the long wooden bar, evokes any number of Hollywood booze flicks, from The Lost Weekend to Days of Wine and Roses. The mood is enhanced by a mellow jazz sound track.

*T*hankfully, the drinks and food at The Screening Room are in no way fifties throwbacks, but rather creative "remakes." The house cocktails include a chipotle chile-fortified Bloody Mary, and Grey Hound, which costars Ketel One vodka and grapefruit juice. Chef Spangenthal puts a twist on McCann's Irish oatmeal with sour cherries and maple sugar, and livens up ever-popular poached eggs on toasted brioche with glazed ham and spinach. His grilled hamburger is one of the city's best (rich, perfectly cooked, and oversized). Other favorites include a hearty baked maccheroni, rich with leeks, tomatoes, and Parmigiano Reggiano cheese, and a refreshing chopped salad loaded with grilled tuna, jicama, and cucumber tossed with a cilantro lime vinaigrette.

*A*fter brunch, move to the intimate screening room with its retro funky feel and groovy lighting. Sink into a comfy seat, and kick back with Audrey or Jackie.

In the Neighborhood

Canal Street shopping, stopping at **Pearl Paint** for all the art supplies you need; **Chinatown** with its restaurants, bustling groceries; Chinese department store extraordinaire, **Pearl River Mart** at Canal and Lafayette Sts., for a silk cheongsam dress, housewares, or exotic gift items.

Tartine

253 WEST 11TH STREET AT WEST 4TH STREET
229-2611
SATURDAYS AND SUNDAYS, 10:30 A.M.—4 P.M.
RESERVATIONS NOT ACCEPTED.
$
CASH ONLY

Tartine's golden, browned-to-perfection apple pancakes have New Yorkers lining up along the tree-lined sidewalk in fair and rainy weather. But that's not the only delicacy on chef Thierry Rochard's eclectic menu. The croissants are extra flaky and buttery, the croque monsieur is extra cheesy, and the pastries—made fresh daily on the premises—-extra rich and fruity. Take the tarte fines aux pommes a la mode: it's a crisp round of puff pastry with delicately sliced apples and a sprinkling of cinnamon, served warm and topped with outrageous homemade vanilla ice cream. It will give you something new to crave.

Tartine is a precious little cafe with plant-filled windows. Because of its intimate size, the best seats are at tables for two, perfect for a tête-a-tête with your best friend. In the spring and summer, there are six choice tables outside.

In the Neighborhood

Bookleaves, a second-hand bookstore just north on West 4th; south on Bleecker St., **Lifevisions** for tarot card readings, and **Hudson St. Papers** for fun.

Thady Con's

915 SECOND AVENUE BET. 48TH
AND 49TH STREETS
688-9700
SATURDAYS AND SUNDAYS, NOON—3:30 P.M.
RESERVATIONS NOT ACCEPTED.
$
AMEX, V, MC

It's Sunday morning and you crave a hearty Irish breakfast. Head for Thady Con's, a pub so Irish that it might have been flown in from Donegal. Walk past real fiddlers who play Irish tunes throughout the afternoon, past the long bar where the regulars hang out, past the mural of fiddlers and into the quaint back room that has been made to resemble a rustic Celtic cottage, right down to mottled, water-stained walls, a fire crackling in the grate, and trompe l'oeil cottage windows that "look out" onto scenes of the rolling countryside.

The menu features dishes hearty enough to satisfy a team of rugby all-stars.

In the Neighborhood

The **United Nations** for a general tour or a stroll through the complex's riverside rose gardens; **Japan Society Gallery** at 47th St. bet. First and Second Aves., for art exhibitions, lectures and a film program; **Tudor City's >**

*B*reakfast for one? A fairly typical order is composed of bacon, sausage, black-and-white blood pudding, baked beans, grilled tomato, and eggs any style, and the traditional Irish dish, boxty, an herbed potato pancake. The kitchen serves up several prix fixe selections that include American brunch standards, but with a Gaelic twist, like eggs Benedict, which is served with brown bread (instead of an English muffin) and Irish bacon; and Buck's Fizz, an Irish mimosa. But for a true taste of Ireland, order a pint of the real stuff—Guinness—and let the blarney commence.

quaint English-style apartment buildings built in the late 1920s; **Grand Central Station's** newly restored ceiling.

The Treehouse

436 HUDSON STREET AT MORTON STREET
989-1363
SATURDAYS, 11 A.M.—4 P.M.;
SUNDAYS, 10 A.M.—4 P.M.
RESERVATIONS ACCEPTED.
$
AMEX, V, MC

*T*he whimsical Treehouse is a children's paradise, complete with a pint-sized desk by the door with storybooks and a cooking setup that allows kids to make their very own chocolate-chip cookies, which are baked while you eat (Sundays only).

*B*oughs of forsythia frame the entrance to an enchanting room decorated with bittersweet, teacups, birdhouses, flowerpots, and a grapevine frieze on soft yellow and lime-green walls. The sweetness extends to the menu, where the specialty of the house is an apple pancake, oven-baked with a pure maple glaze. Sweeter still is cherry-stuffed French toast infused with orange, cinnamon, rum, and vanilla. Eggs Florentine are poached on a biscuit, topped with spinach and mornay sauce, and served with mesclun tossed with a creamy garlic dressing. The Provençal omelet is a savory medley of tomatoes, herbs, fontina cheese, and mushrooms, plated with shallot and garlic green beans.

*L*uncheon and dinner selections available for brunch are grilled fillet of Atlantic salmon, and roast chicken or turkey dinners served home-style, with apple stuffing and natural gravy. Children's portions are available, of course, and include the guaranteed favorites—char-grilled burgers

In the Neighborhood

On the same street, the charming general store **Bespeckled Trout** for fly-fishing paraphernalia and penny candy; **Film Forum** at West Houston near Seventh Ave. So. for a movie classic.

and hot dogs. Kids will also love side
dishes like Southern ham and cured
bacon; and we strongly recommend
the angel hair onion rings, which are
ever-so-delicately   battered and fine
as, well, angel hair.

Triple Eight Palace

EAST BROADWAY MALL, 88 EAST BROADWAY
BET. DIVISION AND MARKET STREETS
941-8886
SATURDAYS AND SUNDAYS, 8 A.M.—4 P.M.
RESERVATIONS NOT ACCEPTED.
$
AMEX, V, MC

im sum, those luscious little
Chinese dumplings, are available at
many restaurants in Chinatown, but
we think frenetic, bustling Triple Eight
Palace sets the standard for the best in
New York. Don't expect to escape the
crowds in the gaudy, multilevel mall
that houses this gargantuan establish-
ment. It's noisy and chaotic, but that's
part of the dim sum experience in
Chinatown.

s you step off the escalator that
ascends from the ground floor, you

may have a lengthy wait before the maitre d', holding a walkie-talkie, leads you to a table. As is typical for a large Chinese restaurant, many of the tables seat eight to ten and are occupied mostly by Asian families. Relax and you'll find yourself easily wrapped up in the goings-on, sipping tea, or, as the Chinese regulars do, ordering a Coke! But don't ask for a menu. Instead, wait for the dim sum carts. They are manned mostly by non-English speaking attendants, who roll them through the restaurant at a rate that may make your head spin. When a cart stops at your table, choose any little dish that looks good and the attendant will stamp it on the bill at your table.

The vegetable dumplings in little steamer baskets are particularly tasty with a crisp celery, corn, carrot, and mushroom filling. The delicate, steamed shrimp balls are exquisite and the shrimp toast delightfully crunchy. The variety is enormous. You'll find turnip cakes, spring rolls, pork dumplings, steamed pork buns, and more. And we've never met a dumpling we didn't like at Triple Eight Palace.

In the Neighborhood

Chinatown in all of its fascinating variety: the multilevel mall that houses **Triple 8** for herbal medicine shops, trinket sellers, and plenty of Hello Kitty! products; fish and vegetable markets along Canal Street;

Chinatown Ice Cream Factory, Bayard St. bet. Mott and Elizabeth Sts., with flavors ranging from green tea to exotic lychee and red bean.

Verbena

54 IRVING PLACE BET. 17TH
AND 18TH STREETS
260-5454
SUNDAYS, 11:30 A.M.—2:30 P.M.
RESERVATIONS SUGGESTED.
$$$
AMEX, V,
MC

At lovely Verbena, just two blocks from Gramercy Park, tables in the jewel-like dining room and luxurious garden are coveted, so be sure to make reservations early, especially during the warm-weather months. Verbena attracts a well-dressed crowd that appreciates the refined, somewhat formal setting and chef Diane Forley's New American cuisine, which is a colorful, healthy mix of fish and meat dishes flavored with herbs and light sauces.

While dinner can be pricey, brunch at Verbena offers an excellent and affordable prix fixe meal that includes choice of a daily soup, mesclun or Caesar salad, and an

In the Neighborhood

Irving Place, with its landmark homes, including one at the northwest corner of 17th St. once occupied by Edith Wharton; at Irving Place and 20th St., famous **Gramercy Park**, with its gated garden; **Saint George's Church** at ➤

entree. We like the fried eggs with whitefish hash, oven-roasted tomato, and watercress; orecchiette with diced tuna, capers, and crunchy haricots verts; and the rich croque monsieur, loaded with smoked Black Forest ham and fontina cheese. Chef Forley's famous popover stuffed with scrambled eggs and caviar is a decadent, delicious choice.

Park Ave. and 21st St., often offering musical programs on weekends.

*A*s you peruse the menu and admire the exquisite surroundings—pressed botanicals, verdant plants, and delicate flowers—consider starting brunch Kentucky-style, with a mint julep, garnished with a sprig of in-house-grown herb and augmented with a potent jigger of Rebel Yell bourbon.

The Vinegar Factory

431 EAST 91ST STREET, 2ND FLOOR,
BET. FIRST AND YORK AVENUES
987-0885
SATURDAYS AND SUNDAYS, 8 A.M.—4 P.M.
RESERVATIONS NOT ACCEPTED.
$
AMEX, V, MC

*N*othing whets your weekend appetite like a walk through a market bursting with a kaleidoscope of gorgeous fruits and vegetables, aromatic cheeses, and fresh breads. Eli Zabar (of Eli's Bread and E.A.T.) has created just such a wonderland of produce, much of which is grown right on the roof of The Vinegar Factory. Brunch, prepared from all this abundance, awaits in the upstairs cafe. Here you will find some of the best French toast in the city made from a thick slice of fresh challah. The roster of salads holds healthful surprises like crunchy wheat berries tossed with toasted veggies, wild rice couscous, and nutty sesame bok choy. Filling, satisfying egg dishes include eggs Benedict presented on a toasted slice of challah, a sweet foil to the rich lemony hollandaise, and a country omelet with cheese, potato, onion, and bacon. Everything comes with plenty

In the Neighborhood

Carl Schurz Park, with **Gracie Mansion**, the mayor's official residence, at the north end, affords a lovely walk along the **East River**.

of Eli's bread and strawberry jam, and, if you like, a fresh berry smoothie on the side.

*W*ith a balloon for every tiny tot, this is a great place to take children. Count on it being packed between noon and 2 P.M. with only about a twenty-minute wait, but if you come early—say, 10:30—you can easily seat a large group.

Zinno

126 West 13th Street bet. Sixth
and Seventh Avenues
924-5182
Sundays, 11:30 a.m.—3:30 p.m.
Reservations accepted.
$$
AmEx, V, MC

What a concept: an Italian restaurant with a floor show of jazz tap dancers and live music! Bear in mind that the seats directly next to the performance area, in the rear of the restaurant, get you right in on the action but can be a bit noisy for conversation. That said, you have only to enjoy Zinno's reliably good Italian food. While there is no charge for the entertainment, there is an $18 minimum on food and beverage.

Sip a glass of champagne or mimosa while enjoying a basket of crusty Italian bread and mint chocolate chip muffins. Although the menu is seasonal, a favorite entree is a Tuscan farmer's breakfast made to order with three eggs, grilled skirt steak or chicken sausage, roasted red peppers, and tomatoes. On the light side is the Italian club sandwich with roasted chicken, prosciutto di Parma, fresh

In the Neighborhood

Two of the best gourmet markets in the city — **Jefferson Market** and **Balducci's** — are on Sixth Ave. bet. 9th and 12th Sts.; adventuresome young artists show at **White Columns**, west on 13th St. (entrance on Horatio St.)

mozzarella, and baby lettuces with just the right splash of oil and vinegar on thinly sliced whole-grain bread. Zinno also offers great pasta. We recommend the artichoke ravioli with a sauce of roasted tomatoes, capers, and ricotta cheese, and the rigatoni with fennel sausage, sun-dried tomatoes, wilted arugula, and spicy tomato sauce. Don't miss Zinno's desserts, which include a rich tiramisu and creamy Italian cheesecake made with ricotta cheese.

*N*ow about those dancers. They tend to take some time off in the summer and resume in September. You'll catch the entire act if you make a reservation for 12:30 P.M. By then the musicians are warmed up and the dancers' feet are happily tapping.

10 Bonus Brunch Spots

Annie's 1381 Third Ave. (bet. 78th and 79th Sts.)
212-327-4853. Popular, family-friendly Upper East Side spot.

Bendix Diner 219 Eighth Ave. (at 21st St.) 212-366-0560.
167 First Ave. (bet. 10th and 11th Sts.) 212-260-4220.
Asia meets America at this Chelsea diner-with-a-twist.

Bubby's 120 Hudson St. (at North Moore) 212-219-0666.
For a down-home brunch, our TriBeCa friends love the hearty
fare at this place.

Café Luxembourg 200 West 70th St. (bet. Amsterdam
and West End Ave.) 212-873-7411.
French bistro fare in a funky La Coupole-like setting.

Dizzy's Diner 819 Eighth Ave. (at 9th St.), Brooklyn
718-499-1966. This popular Park Slope spot calls itself "a finer
diner," and with good reason.

Grove 314 Bleecker St. (at Grove St.) 212-675-9463.
Try to get a table in the garden at this attractive West Village bistro.

Home 20 Cornelia St. (bet. Bleecker and West 4th Sts.)
212-243-9579. Cozy spot with home-cooked favorites; check
out the back garden in warm weather.

Paris Commune 411 Bleecker St. (bet. Bank and West
11th Sts.) 212-929-0509. Popular, intimate restaurant with
simple, country-style classics.

Sylvia's 328 Lenox Ave. (bet. 126th and 127th Sts.)
212-996-0660. A Sunday gospel brunch with great soul food.

The Water Club 500 East 30th St. (at the East River)
212-683-3333. Step aboard this East River barge for a lavish
buffet brunch.

Favorite brunch recipes from

Mesa Grill

Drovers Tap Room

Cafeteria

Petrossian

The Comfort Diner

and Verbena

Spicy Bloody Mary
from Mesa Grill
Serves 2

Ingredients:

8 ounces tomato juice

3 ounces vodka

2 dashes Bobby Flay's hot sauce or Tabasco sauce

1 dash Worcestershire sauce

Pinch of celery salt

Juice of 1 lemon

Ice

Celery stalks for garnish

Combine all ingredients in a small pitcher, pour into 2 large gasses filled with ice, and garnish with celery stalks.

Carrot Nut Muffins
from Drovers Tap Room
Makes 18 muffins

Ingredients:

2 cups all-purpose flour

2 teaspoons baking soda

1 teaspoon cinnamon

1/2 teaspoon ground ginger

1/4 teaspoon ground cloves

1/4 teaspoon kosher salt

1 1/4 cups granulated sugar

2 cups grated carrots

1 Granny Smith apple, peeled and coarsely shredded

1/2 cup finely chopped pecans

3 large eggs

1 cup corn oil

1 tablespoon vanilla extract

Preheat oven to 350.° Place paper muffin liners in 18 muffin cups. Sift the flour, baking soda, cinnamon, ginger, cloves, and salt together in a large bowl. Add the sugar, then stir in the carrots, apples, and pecans. In a separate bowl, whisk together the eggs, oil, and vanilla extract. Add the egg mixture to the flour mixture, stirring just until the batter is combined.

Spoon the batter into prepared muffin cups, filling them 3/4 full. Bake for 10 to 12 minutes, or until a toothpick inserted into the center of the muffin comes out clean. Place muffin pan on a rack and cool for five minutes, then remove from the tins and cool completely on wire rack. Muffins can be stored in airtight container up to 4 days.

Frog in the Hole

from Cafeteria

Serves 4

Ingredients:

4 slices thick-cut wheat bread
1/2 cup clarified butter
4 large eggs
4 vine-ripened tomatoes, sliced
1 medium red onion, sliced thin
2 tablespoons olive oil
2 tablespoons red wine vinegar
Salt and pepper to taste
12 slices smoked salmon

Remove a hole 2 inches in diameter from the center of each slice of bread. (A jelly jar lid works very well as a quick "cutter" for the center.)

In a pancake griddle or a large nonstick pan, over medium heat, heat 2 tablespoons clarified butter. Toast each slice of bread on one side for 3 minutes. Carefully crack an egg through the hole and sauté the egg inside. When the egg sets on one side, but the yolk is still soft, turn the toast over, being careful not to crack the yolk. Add butter to pan as needed. Sauté for 2 minutes more. While the eggs are cooking, season tomato and onion slices with olive oil, red wine vinegar, and salt and pepper in a mixing bowl. To serve, stack tomatoes and onions in corner of each serving plate. Lean the "frog in the hole" against the tomatoes and garnish with a rosette of the 3 slices of smoked salmon.

Paris's Soft Scrambled Eggs With Cream Cheese & Sevruga Caviar

from Petrossian

Serves 4

Ingredients:

1 package (8 ounces) cream cheese, softened
12 eggs
1 container (8 ounces) heavy cream
1 bunch finely chopped chives
60 grams Sevruga caviar
4 bagels
Salt and pepper to taste

Whip cream cheese until fluffy. In a nonstick pan over medium heat, whisk eggs and cream. Add chopped chives and salt and pepper. Cook eggs until just set but soft and moist. Spread half the whipped cream cheese on bottom half of bagels. Divide scrambled eggs over top. On top half of bagel make an egg-shaped quenelle, or ball, of the rest of the cream cheese. Place each half bagel leaning against each other. Garnish scrambled eggs with Sevruga caviar. Serve with green salad, if desired.

Berry-Stuffed French Toast

from Comfort Diner

Serves 6

Ingredients:

1 loaf day-old challah bread

1 pint each blueberries, strawberries, and
   raspberries, mixed

4 eggs

1 1/2 cups milk

1 teaspoon vanilla extract

1 tablespoon granulated sugar

1/4 teaspoon cinnamon

6 tablespoons unsalted butter

Cut bread into six 2-inch slices and cut each slice
in half. Make an incision 2/3 of the way deep and 2/3
wide. Stuff as much of the berry mixture as you can
possibly fit into each pocket. In a large, shallow bowl,
whisk together eggs, milk, vanilla, sugar and cinnamon.
Soak each berry-filled piece of bread in the eggs for 3
minutes, or a little longer if you like custardy French
toast. In a large nonstick skillet over medium heat, melt
1 tablespoon of the butter. Add 1/3 of the bread slices
in a single layer and cook the bread 4 to 5 minutes
until golden brown.

Turn the slices and cook the second side 3 to 4
minutes until golden. Transfer to a cookie sheet and
cover with aluminum foil; keep in an oven on warm
and repeat the process 2 more times until complete.
Serve 2 pieces of berry-stuffed French toast per person
and top with more of the berry mixture.

Croque Monsieur
from **V**erbena
Serves 10

Ingredients:

20 slices white bread, crusts removed
1/2 cup mascarpone cheese
1/4 pound fontina cheese, grated
1/2 pound sliced smoked Black Forest ham
2 tablespoons chopped chives or chive oil
2 cups cream or milk
6 eggs
Salt and pepper to taste
1 tablespoon olive oil

Butter and line 12x4x4 inch loaf pan with parchment paper. Begin layering croque monsieur by lining bottom of prepared pan with bread, using 4 slices for each layer. Use 2 tablespoons mascarpone cheese on the first layer, spreading as evenly as possible. Drizzle chive oil or fresh chives over cheese. Sprinkle with 1/2 cup fontina cheese. Layer ham over cheese. (This is one complete layer.) Build three more complete layers, ending with a row of bread.

Whisk cream (or milk) and eggs together to make a custard. Strain through sieve. Season custard with salt and pepper. Pour custard over layers and let rest at least 2 hours before baking. (The assembled layers can be placed overnight in the refrigerator, if desired.)

Place loaf pan in deep casserole and add water half-way up the sides to create bain-marie, or water bath. Bake at 325° until set, 45 minutes to 1 hour. Test with toothpick. If it comes out clean, remove pan from oven. Let cool in loaf pan. Turn out of pan and cut into 1/2-inch-thick slices.

To serve, heat 8-inch sauté pan with olive oil. Gently place croque monsieur into pan and flip to other side when browned. Serve with green salad, if desired.

For hors d'oeuvres, cut chilled croque monsieur into 1/2-inch sticks and skewer before sautéing in sauté pan.

Price

$	Under $12
$$	$12 to $18
$$$	$19 to $25
$$$$	Over $25

Neighborhood

cont. >

C Types of uisine

cont. >

Types of Cuisine

Special Features

Buffet Brunch
Copeland's   30
La Belle Epoque (Sundays) 53

Country in the City
Cub Room Cafe   32
Danal   33
Drovers Tap Room   35
Good Enough to Eat   45
Kitchenette   52
Popover Cafe   74
Thady Con's   86
Treehouse, The   87

Gardens
Danal   33
Le Jardin Bistro   57
Le Madeleine   58
Verbena   91

Gospel Brunch
Copeland's   30
Lola   64

Jazz Brunch
Blue Water Grill   15
Jules   48
La Belle Epoque   53
Lenox Room   60
Zinno   95

Kid Friendly
Barney Greengrass   13
Comfort Diner, The   28
Drovers Tap Room   35
E.A.T.   38
Fifty-Seven Fifty-Seven   41
French Roast   43
Good Enough to Eat   45
Lola   64
Odeon   70
Petite Abeille   71
Popover Cafe   74
Treehouse, The   87
Triple Eight Palace   89
Vinegar Factory, The   93

Meal and a Museum
Balthazar   11
(Guggenheim SoHo, Museum for African Art, The New Museum)
Cafe M   21
(Metropolitan Museum of Art)
Canal House   24
(Guggenheim SoHo)
E.A.T.   38
(Metropolitan Museum of Art)
La Lunchonette   55
(Dia Center for the Arts)
Lenox Room   60
(The Frick Collection, The Metropolitan Museum of Art)
Popover Cafe   74
(Children's Museum of Manhattan, Museum of Natural History, New York Historical Society)

cont. >

Puttin' on the Ritz

Quiet Places

Romantic Room

Sidewalk Tables

Also from City & Company

You can find these guides at your local bookstore, through booksellers on the web,
or by contacting us directly.

NEW YORK'S 50 BEST SERIES

New York's 50 Best New & Avant-Garde Art Galleries $14.00
New York's 50 Best Bookstores for Booklovers $12.00
New York's 50 Best Places to Go Birding $15.00
New York's 50 Best Places to Discover and Enjoy in Central Park $12.00
New York's 50 Best Places toTake Children $12.00
New York's 50 Best Places to Have a Kid's Party $12.00
New York's 50 Best Museums for Cool Parents and Their Kids $12.00
New York's 75 Best Hot Nightspots $12.00
New York's 100 Best Places to Have a Party $12.00
New York's 50 Best Places to Find Peace & Quiet, 2nd ed. $12.00
New York's 100 Best Little Places to Shop $14.00
New York's 50 Best Skyscrapers $12.00
New York's 50 Best Places to Eat Southern $12.00
New York's 60 Best Wonderful Little Hotels, 2nd ed. $15.00

City & Company
22 West 23rd Street
New York, NY 10010
tel: 212.366.1988
fax: 212.242.0415
e-mail: cityco@bway.net

City & Company
can create a customized reprint
to suit your business and
marketing needs.

About the Authors

Ann Volkwein is Assistant Culinary Director at the Television Food Network. She is also the Manhattan Correspondent for *Hamptons* magazine. When she is not eating her way around the city, she can be found sailing on the Sound or spicing up Explorers Club menus.

Jason Oliver Nixon is the editor-in-chief of both *Hamptons* and *Ocean Drive's Palm Beach* magazines. A former producer at the Television Food Network, Nixon contributes food and travel pieces to *Paper, Travel & Leisure, Condé Nast Traveler* and *sidewalk.com.*

About the Illustrator

Madeline Sorel, a Rhode Island School of Design graduate, lives by the beach in Brooklyn with her husband, two daughters and a dog.

Acknowledgements

Thanks to my mother, Lindley Kirksey, for her insatiable curiosity and to my father, Edward Volkwein, for sharing with me a love of great restaurants. Thanks to Ari Ellis for the inches on his belly and to all my friends who ate eggs benedict after French toast after eggs benedict. And I am forever grateful for the sisterhood of the culinary pod.   Ann Volkwein

Thanks to Lois, Jary, Jennifer and Justin Nixon and Karen Burnham for their ever-present, ever-needed support. A special nod, too, to Mary Grace Cash Sandler for instilling in me a love for the written word, to Julia Roper for taking me under wing when it mattered, and to Christine Muhlke at *Paper* for that first food assignment.   Jason Oliver Nixon